Shiv Chalisa
शिव चालीसा

Om
SHAKTI
An Imprint of Om Books International

Reprinted in 2026

Om SHAKTI An Imprint of Om Books International

Corporate & Editorial Office
A-12, Sector 64, Noida 201 301
Uttar Pradesh, India
Phone: +91 120 477 4100
Email: editorial@ombooks.com
Website: www.ombooksinternational.com

Sales Office
107, Ansari Road, Darya Ganj,
New Delhi 110 002, India
Phone: +91 11 4000 9000
Email: sales@ombooks.com
Website: www.ombooks.com

ISBN: 978-81-1975-009-2

Printed in India

10 9 8 7 6 5

भूमिका

शिव चालीसा भगवान शिव की सुंदर स्तुति है, जिसमें उनके दिव्य गुणों का वर्णन किया गया है। भगवान शिव, जिन्हें 'महादेव' और 'भोलेनाथ' भी कहा जाता है, त्रिदेवों में संहारक रूप वाले माने जाते हैं। शिव चालीसा का नियमित पाठ करने से भक्तों को मानसिक शांति, धैर्य एवं साहस मिलता है और साथ ही भगवान शिव की आराधना होती है। इसके पाठ से साधक के जीवन में सकारात्मक ऊर्जा का संचार होता है, जिससे उसे सभी प्रकार के कष्टों और संकटों से मुक्ति मिलती है। विशेष रूप से सोमवार के दिन शिव चालीसा का पाठ करने से भगवान शिव की कृपा शीघ्र प्राप्त होती है, क्योंकि यह दिन उन्हें बहुत प्रिय है।

Introduction

Shiv Chalisa is a beautiful hymn dedicated to Lord Shiva, describing his divine qualities. Lord Shiva, also known as 'Mahadev' and 'Bholenath', is considered the destroyer among the three principal deities (Trimurti). Regular recitation of the Shiv Chalisa provides devotees with mental peace, patience, and courage, and it also serves as an act of worship to Lord Shiva. The recitation of this Chalisa generates positive energy in the devotee's life, freeing them from all kinds of suffering and troubles. Reciting the Shiv Chalisa, especially on Mondays quickly brings the grace of Lord Shiva, as this day is very dear to him.

Shiv Chalisa
शिव चालीसा

।। दोहा ।।

श्री गणेश गिरिजा सुवन, मंगल मूल सुजान।
कहत अयोध्यादास, देहु अभय वरदान।।

ShriGaneshGirijaasuvan,mangalmoolsujaan
Kahat Ayodhyadas tum dehu abhay varadaan

हे गिरिजा पुत्र, भगवान श्री गणेश आपकी जय हो। आप मंगल के मूल आधार एवं बुद्धिविधाता हैं। अयोध्यादास आपसे निडरता का वरदान माँगता है।

Oh son of Girija, Lord Ganesha victory to you. You are the fundamental basis of auspiciousness and the bestower of wisdom. Ayodhyadas seeks a boon of fearlessness from you.

।। चौपाई ।।

जय गिरिजा पति दीन दयाला।
सदा करत सन्तन प्रतिपाला।। 1 ।।

Jai Girijaa pati deendayaalaa
Sada karat santan pratipaalaa

हे गिरिजा पति, हे दीन हीन पर दया बरसाने वाले भगवान शिव, आपकी जय हो, आप सदैव संतों का पालन करते हैं।

O Glorious Lord, husband of Parvati, you are most kind. You always bless your pious devotees.

भाल चन्द्रमा सोहत नीके।
कानन कुण्डल नागफनी के।। 2।।

Bhaal chandramaa sohat neekay
Kaanan kundal naagphani kay

आपके मस्तक पर छोटा-सा चंद्रमा शोभायमान है, आपने कानों में नागफनी के कुण्डल धारण किए हुए हैं।

You are adorned with the moon on your forehead and the hoods of snakes form your earrings.

अंग गौर शिर गंग बहाये।
मुण्डमाल तन छार लगाये।। 3।।

Ang gaur shir gang bahaahye
Mundmaal tan chhaar lagaaye

आप गौर वर्ण के हैं। आपकी जटाओं से गंगा बहती है। आपके गले में नरमुण्डों की माला है और तन पर भस्म लगी हुई है।

You are fair complexioned. The holy River Ganga flows down your matted hair. You wear a garland of skulls around your neck and ash is smeared on your whole body.

वस्त्र खाल बाघम्बर सोहे।
छवि को देख नाग मुनि मोहे।। 4।।

Vastra khaal baaghambar sohay
Chhavi ko dekh naag muni mohay

बाघ की खाल के वस्त्र आप पर जँच रहे हैं। आपकी छवि को देखकर नाग तथा मुनि भी आकर्षित होते हैं।

The tiger skin you wrap around your body looks attractive and pleases the serpents and the saints alike.

मैना मातु की ह्वै दुलारी।
बाम अंग सोहत छवि न्यारी।। 5।।

Mainaa maatu ki hvai dulaari
Vaam ang sohat chhavi nyaari

माता मैना की लाडली पुत्री आपके बायें अंग में आपकी पत्नी के रूप में सुशोभित हैं।

O Lord, the beloved daughter of Mainaa seated on your left as your consort presents a splendid sight.

कर त्रिशूल सोहत छवि भारी।
करत सदा शत्रुन क्षयकारी।। 6।।

Kar trishool sohat chhavi bhaari
Karat sadaa shatrun kshaykaari

आपके हाथों में त्रिशूल आपकी छवि को अत्यधिक सुंदर बनाता है। आपने सदैव शत्रुओं का विध्वंस किया है।

The splendid trident that graces your hand, destroys all enemies.

नंदी गणेश सोहै तहँ कैसे।
सागर मध्य कमल हैं जैसे।। 7।।

Nandi Ganesh sohey tahan kaise
Saagar madhya kamal hain jaise

आपके सानिध्य में नंदी व गणेश जल के बीच खिले दो कमलों के समान सुंदर दिखाई देते हैं।

In your proximity, Nandi and Ganesha appear as resplendent as two lotuses blooming in the water.

कार्तिक श्याम और गणराऊ।
या छवि को कहि जात न काऊ।। 8।।

Kaartik shyaam aur ganaraaoo
Ya chhavi ko kahi jaat na kaaoo

आपके साथ कार्तिकेय तथा गणों की छवि की शोभा अवर्णनीय है।

The beautiful spectacle of Kaartikeya and the ganas present with you is indescribable.

देवन जबहीं जाय पुकारा।
तब ही दुख प्रभु आप निवारा।। 9।।

Devan jabahi jaaye pukaara
Tabahi dukh prabhu aap nivaara

देवताओं ने जब भी आपको सहायता के लिए पुकारा है,
आपने तुरंत उनके दुःखों का निवारण किया है।

O Lord, whenever the deities humbly pray to you for your help, you kindly and graciously resolve all their sorrows.

किया उपद्रव तारक भारी।
देवन सब मिलि तुमहिं जुहारी।। 10।।

Kiyaa upadrav Taarak bhaari
Devan sab mili tumahi juhaari

तारकासुर जैसे राक्षस ने बहुत उत्पात मचाया, तब परेशान देवताओं ने आपकी शरण में आकर आपसे रक्षा करने की प्रार्थना की।

When the demon Taarakasur created havoc in their lives, the gods prayed to you for protection.

तुरत षडानन आप पठायउ।
लवनिमेष महँ मारि गिरायउ।। 11।।

Turat Shadaanan aap patthaayou
Lavanimesh mahan maari giraayou

हे प्रभु! आपने तारकासुर को मारने के लिए षडानन(छह मुखी कार्तिकेय) को तुरंत वहाँ भेजा।

O Lord, you sent Shadaanan (the six-faced Kaartikeya) without delay who at once slayed the evil demon.

आप जलंधर असुर संहारा।
सुयश तुम्हार विदित संसारा।। 12।।

Aap Jalandhar asur sanhaara
Suyash tumhaar vidit sansaara

आपने ही जलंधर नामक राक्षस
का वध किया।
आपके इस कल्याणकारी यश को
पूरा संसार जानता है।

You also killed the demon Jalandhara.
The whole world is aware of your fame.

त्रिपुरासुर सन युद्ध मचाई।
सबहिं कृपा कर लीन बचाई।। 13।।

Tripuraasur san yudhh machaayee
Sabahi kripaa kar leen bachaayee

सभी पर कृपा बरसाते हुए आपने
त्रिपुरासुर के साथ युद्ध करके देवताओं के
प्राणों की रक्षा की।

You saved all gods and humans by defeating and killing the Tripuraasuras (trio of demon brothers).

किया तपहिं भागीरथ भारी।
पुरब प्रतिज्ञा तसु पुरारी।। 14।।

Kiya tapahin Bhaagirath bhaari
Purba pratigya tasu puraari

भागीरथ के तप से प्रसन्न होकर आपने उनकी अपने पूर्वजों की आत्माओं को शांति प्रदान करने की प्रतिज्ञा पूर्ण करने में सहायता की(अपनी जटाओं से गंगा को मुक्त किया)।

Pleased with his tough penance, you helped Bhaagirath in the salvation of the souls of his dead ancestors(by releasing the Ganga who was locked up in your matted hair).

दानिन महँ तुम सम कोउ नाहीं।
सेवक स्तुति करत सदाहीं।। 15।।

Daanin mahan tum sum kou naahin
Sevak stuti karat sadaahin

आपके समान दानी कोई अन्य नहीं है।
भक्त और सेवक सर्वदा आपका गुणगान
करते रहते हैं।

There is no one as charitable as you.
Devotees always sing your glory.

वेद नाम महिमा तव गाई।
अकथ अनादि भेद नहिं पाई।। 16।।

Ved naam mahimaa tab gaaee
Akath anaadi bhed nahin paaee

वेदों ने भी आपकी महिमा का व्याख्यान किया है। पर आपका न आदि है न अंत जिस कारण आपका भेद कोई नहीं जान सका है।

The Vedas have sung your glory but no one has been able to solve the mystery of your origin since you have no beginning nor end, and hence are eternal.

प्रकटी उदधि मंथन में ज्वाला।
जरे सुरासुर भये विहाला।। 17।।

Prakati udadhi manthan mein jwaala
Jaray surasur bhaye vihaala

जब क्षीर सागर के मंथन में विष से भरा पात्र प्रकट हुआ तो सभी देवता व दानव भय से थरथराते हुए उसकी ज्वाला में जलने लगे।

When the deadly poison emerged during the churning of the ocean, gods and demons all trembled with fear and began to burn in the intense heat.

कीन्ह दया तहँ करी सहाई।
नीलकण्ठ तब नाम कहाई।। 18।।

Keenh dayaa tahan karee sahaaee
Neelakanth tab naam kahaaee

आपने ही सब पर दया करते हुए इस विष को अपने कंठ में धारण करके सबकी सहायता की, जिससे आपका नाम नीलकंठ पड़ा।

Taking pity on their plight, you drank the poison and held it in your throat which turned blue. Then you were named Neelakanttha or the blue-throated one.

पूजन रामचंद्र जब कीन्हा।
जीत के लंक विभीषण दीन्हा।। 19।।

Poojan Ramchandra jab keenha
Jeet ke Lanka Vibheeshana deenha

राक्षसों से युद्ध करने से पूर्व जब भगवान श्रीरामचंद्र ने आपकी आराधना की, तभी वे लंका पर विजय प्राप्त कर उसे विभीषण को सौंपने में सफल हुए।

After Lord Rama worshipped you, he was able to gain victory over Lanka and hand over the kingdom to Vibheeshana.

सहस कमल में हो रहे धारी।
कीन्ह परीक्षा तबहिं पुरारी।। 20।।

Sahas kamal me ho rahe dhaari
Keenh pareekshaa tabahin puraari

जब श्रीराम पूजा करते हुए आपकी
सेवा में सहस्त्र कमल अर्पण कर रहे थे,
तब आपने उनकी परीक्षा ली।

When Shri Rama wished to worship
you with one thousand lotus flowers,
you tested his devotion.

एक कमल प्रभु राखेउ जोई।
कमल नयन पूजन चहं सोई।। 21।।

Ek kamal prabhu raakheyu joee
Kamal nayan poojan chaha soee

श्रीराम की परीक्षा लेते हुए आपने एक कमल को छुपा लिया। अपनी पूजा को पूरा करने के लिए भगवान राम ने कमल के स्थान पर अपने नेत्र से पूजा संपन्न करने की ठानी।

O Lord, you hid one of those lotus flowers to test his devotion. Then Shri Ram thought of offering his lotus-like eyes to worship you.

कठिन भक्ति देखी प्रभु शंकर।
भये प्रसन्न दिये इच्छित वर।। 22।।

Katthin bhakti dekhi Prabhu Shankar
Bhaye prasanna diye ichchhit var

श्रीराम की कठिन भक्ति और दृढ़ आस्था देखकर भगवान शंकर ने प्रसन्न होकर उनको मनचाहा वरदान प्रदान किया।

Pleased with his intense devotion, Lord Shankar granted Shri Rama his desired boon.

जय जय जय अनंत अविनाशी।
करत कृपा सबके घटवासी।। 23।।

Jai jai jai anant avinaashi
Karat kripa sabke ghat vaasi

जिनका न आदि है, न अंत है, जो अविनाशी हैं,
और सबके हृदय में वास करके कृपा बरसाते हैं,
उन भगवान शिव की जय हो।

Victory be upon the eternal, indestructible Lord Shiva who resides in the hearts of all his devotees and showers his blessings upon them.

दुष्ट सकल नित मोहि सतावै।
भ्रमत रहे मोहि चैन न आवै।। 24।।

Dusht sakal nit mohi sataavey
Bhramat rahe mohi chaiyn na aavey

काम, क्रोध, मोह, लोभ, अहंकार जैसे सभी दुष्ट विचार मुझे सताते रहते हैं। इन्होंने मुझे भ्रमित कर दिया है, जिससे मुझे कहीं भी शांति नहीं मिल पाती है।

Evil thoughts constantly trouble my mind. They have misguided me and I have lost my peace of mind.

त्रहि त्रहि मैं नाथ पुकारो।
यहि अवसर मोहि आन उबारो।। 25।।

Trahi-trahi main naath pukaaro
Yahi avasar mohi aan ubaaro

हे नाथ, मेरी रक्षा करो और मुझे मोहमाया से
मुक्त करके सांसारिक कष्टों से उबारो।

O Lord, I request you to free me from the bondage of wordly desires and protect me.

लै त्रिशूल शत्रुन को मारो।
संकट से मोहि आन उबारो।। 26।।

Ley trishool shatrun ko maaro
Sankat se mohi aan ubaaro

अपने त्रिशूल से सभी शत्रुओं का नाश करके
मुझे इन कष्टों से मुक्ति दिलाओ और
भवसागर से पार लगाओ।

Destroy my enemies with your trident
and protect me from all danger.

मातु पिता भ्राता सब होई।
संकट में पूछत नहिं कोई।। 27।।

Maatu pitaa bhraata sab hoyee
Sankat mein poochhat nahin koyee

माता-पिता, भाई-बंधु, संबंधी सब होते हैं,
लेकिन संकट के समय सब मुँह मोड़ लेते हैं।

Parents, siblings and loved ones are all present in my life but when I am in distress, no one is there to help me.

स्वामी एक है आस तुम्हारी।
आय हरहु अब संकट भारी।। 28।।

Swaami ek hai aas tumhaari
Aaye harahu ab sankat bhaari

हे स्वामी, मुझे केवल आपकी ही आस है, आप पर विश्वास है। आप आकर मेरे कष्टों और संकटों को दूर कर दो।

O Lord, You are my only hope. Please eliminate the grave problems and sufferings in my life.

धन निर्धन को देत सदाहीं।
जो कोई जाँचे वो फल पाहीं।। 29।।

Dhan nirdhan ko det sadaa hee
Jo koi jaanche so phal paaheen

आप सदा ही दीन-हीनों की सहायता करते हैं। आप अपने भक्तों को मनचाहा वरदान प्रदान करते हैं।

You always come to the rescue of the needy. You grant their desired boons.

अस्तुति केहि विधि करौं तुम्हारी।
क्षमहु नाथ अब चूक हमारी।। 30।।

Astuti kehi vidhi karauon tumhaari
Kshamahu naath ab chook hamaari

हम आपकी स्तुति, आपकी प्रार्थना किस विधि से करें, यह हमें ज्ञात नहीं है। प्रभु, अगर आपकी पूजा करने में कोई चूक हुई हो, तो हमें क्षमा कर देना।

I do not know the proper rituals by which to worship you. Please forgive any lapse that has occurred on my part while praying to you.

शंकर हो संकट के नाशन।
मंगल कारण विघ्न विनाशन।। 31 ।।

Shankar ho sankat ke naashan
Mangal kaaran vighn vinaashan

हे शिव शंकर, आप तो संकटों का विनाश करने वाले हैं। आप भक्तों का कल्याण करने वाले व बाधाओं को दूर हटाने वाले हैं।

O Lord Shankar, You are the destroyer of all miseries. You eliminate all obstacles and grant your devotees eternal bliss.

योगी यति मुनि ध्यान लगावैं।
नारद शारद शीश नवावैं।। 32।।

Yogi yati muni dhyaan lagaavain
Naarad Shaarad sheesh navaavain

योगी, यति, ऋषि, मुनि सब आपका ध्यान करते हैं। देवी सरस्वती, नारद, आदि, सब आपको नमन करते हैं।

The saints and sages meditate upon your most beautiful form. Even celestial beings like Narad Muni and Goddess Saraswati bow before you.

नमो नमो जय नमो शिवाय।
सुर ब्रह्मादिक पार न पाय।। 33।।

Namo namo jai namah Shivaaye
Sur Brahmaadik paar na paaye

हे भोलेनाथ, आपको नमन है। आपका रहस्य ब्रह्मा, आदि, सभी देवता नहीं समझ सके।

O Lord Shiva, Victory to you whose mystery even Lord Brahma and other gods have not been able to decipher.

जो यह पाठ करे मन लाई।
ता पर होत है शम्भु सहाई।। 34।।

Jo yaha paatth kare mana laaee
Ta par hot hai Shambhu sahaee

जो भी भक्त इस चालीसा का हृदय से पाठ करता है, उसकी भगवान शिव सदैव सहायता करते हैं।

Whoever chants the Shiv Chalisa wholeheartedly receives the blessings of the Lord.

ऋृनिया जो कोई हो अधिकारी।
पाठ करे सो पावन हारी।। 35।।

Riniya jo koi ho adhikaari
Paatth karai so paavan haari

पवित्र मन से इस पाठ को करने से भगवान शिव ऋण में डूबे को ऋण मुक्त कर देते हैं।

Devotees who chant these verses with devotion become free from debt by the grace of Lord Shiva.

पुत्रहीन कर इच्छा कोई।
निश्चय शिव प्रसाद तेहि होई।। 36।।

Putraheen ichchha kar koyee
Nishchay Shiv prasad tehi hoyee

यदि कोई संतानहीन हो तो यह पाठ करने से उसकी इच्छा को भी भगवान शिव का प्रसाद निश्चित रूप से मिलता है।

A childless person praying to Lord Shiva is certainly assured of Shiva's blessing and begets a child.

पण्डित त्रयोदशी को लावे।
ध्यान पूर्वक होम करावे।। 37।।

Pandit trayodashi ko laavey
Dhyaan-poorvak homa karaavey

त्रयोदशी तिथि को पंडित को बुलवाकर हवन करवाना चाहिए।

One should invite a pandit on Trayodashi (Thirteenth day of the lunar fortnight) and devoutly make offerings to Lord Shiva.

त्रयोदशी ब्रत करे हमेशा।
तन नहीं ताके रहे कलेशा।। 38।।

Trayodashi brat kare hameshaa
Tan nahin taake rahe kaleshaa

त्रयोदशी का व्रत रखने से किसी भी प्रकार का कष्ट नहीं रहता और सभी क्लेश दूर हो जाते हैं।

Those who devotedly fast and pray to Lord Shiva on Trayodashi are always healthy and prosperous.

धूप दीप नैवेद्य चढ़ावे।
शंकर सम्मुख पाठ सुनावे।। 39।।

Dhoop deep naivaidya charhaavey
Shankar sanmukh paath sunaavey

धूप-दीप और नैवेद्य से पूजा करके शिवजी की मूर्ति के सामने बैठकर शिव चालीसा का श्रद्धापूर्वक पाठ करना चाहिए।

One must burn incense sticks, light an oil lamp and offer prasad to Lord Shiva and recite the Shiv Chalisa.

जन्म जन्म के पाप नसावे।
अन्त धाम शिवपुर में पावे।। 40।।

Janam janam ke paap nasaavey
Ant dhaam Shivapur me paavey

इससे जन्म-जन्मांतर के पाप समाप्त हो जाते हैं और अंत में मनुष्य शिव के लोक में वास करने लगता है अर्थात् मुक्त हो जाता है।

One who prays to Lord Shiva, enjoys material happiness and spiritual bliss in this world and hereafter ascends to the abode of Lord Shiva.

।। दोहा।।

कहैं अयोध्यादास आस तुम्हारी।
जानि सकल दुःख हरहु हमारी।।

Kahain Ayodhyadaas aas tumhaari
Jaani sakal dukh harahu hamaari

अयोध्यादासजी कहते हैं कि शंकर भगवान, हमें आपसे ही आशा है। आप हमारी मनोकामनाएँ पूरी करके हमारे दुःखों को दूर करें।

Ayodhyadaas says that O Lord Shiva, I have hope only in you. Please remove all my sorrows and sufferings.

।। दोहा ।।

नित्त नेम कर प्रातः ही, पाठ करौं चालीसा।
तुम मेरी मनोकामना, पूर्ण करो जगदीशा।।
मगसर छठि हेमन्त ऋतु, संवत चौसठ जान।
अस्तुति चालीसा शिवहि, पूर्ण कीन कल्याण।।

Nitt nem kari Praatah hee, Paath karow Chalisa
Tum meri manokaamnaa, poorna karo Jagadeesha
Magsar chhathi hemant ritu, samvat chousath jaan
Astuti chaleesa Shivahi, poorn keen kalyaan

प्रतिदिन नियम से उठकर प्रातःकाल शिव चालीसा का पाठ करें और भगवान शंकर जो इस जगत के ईश्वर हैं, उनसे अपनी इच्छा पूरी करने की प्रार्थना करें। संवत 64 में मृगशर मास की छठी तिथि और हेमंत ऋतु में भगवान शिव की स्तुति में शिव चालीसा लोगों के कल्याण के लिए पूर्ण की गई।

O Universal Lord, every morning, I recite this Chalisa with devotion. Please bless me so that I may be able to accomplish my material and spiritual desires. The Shiva Chalisa which was written for the benefit of mankind was completed on the 6th day of the mrigshir month of the samvat 64 in the Hemant (winter) season.

आरती

ॐ जय शिव ओंकारा, स्वामी जय शिव ओंकारा।
ब्रह्मा, विष्णु, सदाशिव, अर्द्धांगी धारा।।
ॐ जय शिव ओंकारा।।

एकानन चतुरानन पंचानन राजे। स्वामी पंचानन राजे।
हंसासन गरूड़ासन वृषवाहन साजे।।
ॐ जय शिव ओंकारा।।

दो भुज चार चतुर्भुज दस भुज अति सोहे। प्रभु दस भुज अति सोहे।
त्रिगुण रूप निरखते, त्रिभुवन जन मोहे।।
ॐ जय शिव ओंकारा।।

अक्षमाला वनमाला रूण्डमाला धारी।
चंदन मृगमद सोहे भाले शशिधारी।।
ॐ जय शिव ओंकारा।।

श्वेताम्बर पीताम्बर बाघम्बर अंगे। स्वामी बाघम्बर अंगे।
सनकादिक गरूणादिक भूतादिक संगे।।
ॐ जय शिव ओंकारा।।

कर के मध्य कमंडलु चक्र त्रिशूल धर्ता। स्वामी चक्र त्रिशूल धर्ता।
जगकर्ता जगभर्ता जगसंहारकर्ता।।
ॐ जय शिव ओंकारा।।

ब्रह्मा विष्णु सदाशिव जानत अविवेका। स्वामी जानत अविवेका।
प्रणवाक्षर में शोभित ये तीनों एका।।
ॐ जय शिव ओंकारा।।

त्रिगुण स्वामी जी की आरती जो कोई नर गावे। प्रभु प्रेम सहित गावे।
कहत शिवानन्द स्वामी, मनवांछित फल पावे।।
ॐ जय शिव ओंकारा।।

Arti

Om Jai Shiv Omkara, Swaamee jai Shiv Omkara,
Brahma, Vishnu, Sadashiv, ardhaangee dhaaraa.
Om Jai Shiv Omkara.

Ekaanan Chaturanan Panchaanan raaje,
Swaamee Panchaanan raaje,
Hansaanan garudasan vrishvaahan saaje.
Om Jai Shiv Omkara.

Do bhuj chaar chatur bhuj dasa bhuj ati sohe,
Swaamee dashabhuj ati sohe,
Trigun roop nirakhate, tribhuvan jan mohe.
Om Jai Shiv Omkara.

Akshamaalaa vanamaalaa rundamaalaa dhaaree,
Chandan mrigamad sohey bhaaley shashidhaaree,
Om Jai Shiv Omkara.

Shvetaambar peetaambar baaghambar angey,
Swaamee baaghambar angey.
Sankadik garunadik bhootadik sangey.
Om Jai Shiv Omkara.

Kar ke madhya kamandalu chakra trishooldhartaa,
Swaamee chakra trishooldhartaa.
Jagkartaa jagbhartaa jagsanhaarkartaa.
Om Jai Shiv Omkara.

Brahma, Vishnu, Sadashiv, jaanat avivekaa,
Swaamee jaanat avivekaa.
Pranavaakshar mein sobhit ye teenon ekaa.
Om Jai Shiv Omkara.

Trigun swaamee jee kee aarti jo koyee nar gaavai,
Prabhu prem sahit gaavai.
Kahat Shivanand Swaamee, Manvanchhit phal paave.
Om Jai Shiv Omkara.

भगवान शिव के 108 नाम

1. शिव : जो परम पवित्र हैं
2. महेश्वर : देवों के ईश्वर
3. शंभवे : समृद्धि के दाता
4. पिनाकिन : पिनाक नामक धनुष धारण करने वाले
5. शशिशेखर : शीश पर चन्द्रमा धारण करने वाले
6. वामदेव : जो हर प्रकार से शुभ एवं सुंदर हैं
7. विरूपाक्ष : तिर्यक नेत्रों वाले
8. कपर्दी : जटा धारण करने वाले
9. नीललोहित : नील और लाल वर्ण वाले
10. शंकर : सुख और समृद्धि के दाता
11. शूलपाणि : त्रिशूल धारण करने वाले
12. खटवांगी : खट्वांग नामक आयुध धारण करने वाले
13. विष्णुवल्लभ : जो भगवान विष्णु को अति प्रिय हैं
14. शिपिविष्ट : प्रकाश की किरणों से व्याप्त

15. अंबिकानाथ : माता अंबिका या पार्वती के प्रभु या पति

16. श्रीकण्ठ : सुंदर कण्ठ वाले

17. भक्तवत्सल : भक्तों पर स्नेह एवं करुणा बरसाने वाले

18. भव : स्वयं प्रकट होने वाले

19. शर्व : समस्त कष्टों एवं पापों को नष्ट करने वाले

20. त्रिलोकेश : तीनों लोकों के स्वामी एवं अधिपति

21. शितिकण्ठ : श्वेत कंठ वाले

22. शिवाप्रिय : पार्वती के प्रिय

23. उग्र : अत्यंत भयंकर प्रकृति वाले

24. कपाली : गले में कपाल की माला धारण करने वाले

25. कामारी : कामदेव को भस्म करने वाले

26. अंधकासुर सूदन : अन्धकासुर का वध करने वाले

27. गंगाधर : जटाओं में देवी गंगा को धारण करने वाले

28.	ललाटाक्ष	: जिनके ललाट पर तीसरा नेत्र है
29.	कालकाल	: जो काल के भी काल हैं
30.	कृपानिधि	: भक्तों पर कृपा करने वाले, कृपा के सागर
31.	भीम	: विशालकाय शरीर वाले
32.	परशुहस्त	: परशु नामक अस्त्र को हाथ में धारण करने वाले
33.	मृगपाणि	: हाथ में नर मृग धारण करने वाले
34.	जटाधर	: जटाधारी शिवजी
35.	कैलाशवासी	: कैलाश पर्वत पर निवास करने वाले
36.	कवची	: विभिन्न प्रकार के आयुध धारण करने वाले
37.	कठोर	: शक्तिशाली शरीर वाले
38.	त्रिपुरान्तक	: त्रिपुरासुर का वध करने वाले
39.	वृषांक	: जिनके ध्वज पर वृष (नन्दी) का चिह्न अंकित है
40.	वृषभारूढ़	: जो नन्दी पर सवार हैं

41. भस्मोद्धूलितविग्रह

: शरीर पर भस्म धारण करने वाले

42. सामप्रिय : जिन्हें समानता प्रिय है

43. स्वरमयी : जो संगीत में पारंगत हैं।

44. त्रयीमूर्ति : जो त्रिमूर्ति (ब्रह्मा, विष्णु, महेश) में से एक हैं/जो ऋग्वेद, सामवेद एवं यजुर्वेद के रूप में स्थित हैं

45. अनीश्वर : जिनका कोई ईश्वर नहीं

46. सर्वज्ञ : जो सब जानते हैं

47. परमात्मा : हर किसी की आत्मा में निवास करने वाले

48. सोमसूर्याग्निलोचन

: चन्द्र, सूर्य एवं अग्नि को अपने तीन नेत्रों के रूप में धारण करने वाले

49. हवि : जो हवन में आहुति के रूप में दिये जाने वाले द्रव्य स्वरूप हैं

50. यज्ञमय : जो स्वयं यज्ञ स्वरूप हैं

51. सोम : जो चन्द्रमा के समान शीतल एवं निर्मल हैं
52. पंचवक्त्र : पाँच मुखों वाले
53. सदाशिव : जो सदैव शुभता के प्रतीक हैं
54. विश्वेश्वर : संपूर्ण विश्व के स्वामी
55. वीरभद्र : जो उग्र एवं शान्त हैं
56. गणनाथ : गणों के स्वामी
57. प्रजापति : समस्त प्राणियों के सृजनकर्ता
58. हिरण्यरेता : किरणों के उद्भवकर्ता
59. दुर्धर्ष : जो अपराजित हैं
60. गिरीश : पर्वतों के ईश्वर
61. गिरिश : कैलाश पर्वत पर शयन करने वाले
62. अनघ : जो पवित्र हैं
63. भुजंगभूषण : सर्पों को आभूषण रूप में धारण करने वाले
64. भर्ग : समस्त पापों का नाश करने वाले
65. गिरिधन्वा : मेरु पर्वत को अपने धनुष के रूप में धारण करने वाले

66. गिरिप्रिय : जिन्हें पर्वत अति प्रिय हैं⁄ जिन्हें देवी पार्वती अत्यन्त प्रिय हैं

67. कृत्तिवासा : बाघम्बर धारण करने वाले

68. पुराराति : त्रिपुरासुर एवं उनके त्रिपुरों (लोकों) का संहार करने वाले

69. भगवान् : जो सर्वशक्तिमान ईश्वर हैं

70. प्रमथाधिप : प्रमथगणों (शिवगणों) के अधिपति

71. मृत्युंजय : मृत्यु पर विजय प्राप्त करने वाले

72. सूक्ष्मतनु : सूक्ष्म देह धारण करने वाले

73. जगद्व्यापी : जो समस्त जगत् में व्याप्त हैं

74. जगद्गुरु : जो संपूर्ण विश्व के गुरु हैं

75. व्योमकेश : जिनके केश समस्त आकाश में व्याप्त हैं

76. महासेनजनक : जो कार्तिकेय के पिता हैं

77. चारुविक्रम : सुन्दरता को जीतने वाले

78. रुद्र : भक्तों के कष्ट से द्रवित होने वाले

79. भूतपति : पंचमहाभूतों या भूतों के स्वामी

80. स्थाणु : जो अडिग एवं अटल हैं

81. अहिर्बुध्न्य : जो समस्त सृष्टि का आधार हैं/कुण्डलिनी धारण करने वाले

82. दिगम्बर : ब्रह्माण्ड को वस्त्र के रूप में धारण करने वाले

83. अष्टमूर्ति : आठ रूपों वाले

84. अनेकात्मा : विविधरूप धारण करने वाले

85. सात्विक : असीमित ऊर्जा के स्वामी

86. शुद्धविग्रह : जो पूर्णतः शुद्ध एवं निर्मल हैं

87. शाश्वत : जो अनन्त एवं अविनाशी हैं

88. खण्डपरशु : खण्डित परशु धारण करने वाले

89. अज : जो अजन्मे, असीमित एवं अजेय हैं

90. पाशविमोचन : सभी सांसरिक बन्धनों से मुक्त करने वाले

91. मृड : सुख-सौभाग्य प्रदान करने वाले

92. पशुपति : समस्त पशुओं के स्वामी

93. देव : जो सर्वशक्तिशाली सर्वव्यापी ईश्वर हैं

94. महादेव : जो देवों के भी देव हैं

95. अव्यय : जो अपरिवर्तनीय हैं

96. हरि : समस्त पापों को हरने वाले

97. भगनेत्रभिद् : भग का नेत्र क्षतिग्रस्त करने वाले

98. अव्यक्त : जो अप्रत्यक्ष हैं

99. दक्षाध्वरहर : दक्ष प्रजापति के यज्ञ का विध्वंस करने वाले

100. हर : समस्त पाप बन्धनों को नष्ट करने वाले

101. पूषदन्तभित् : पूषन नामक देव के दाँत तोड़ने वाले

102. अव्यग्र : स्थिर एवं अटल स्वभाव वाले

103. सहस्त्राक्ष : सहस्त्र नेत्रों वाले

104. सहस्त्रपाद : सहस्त्र पैरों वाले

105. अपवर्गप्रद : मोक्ष प्रदान करने वाले

106. अनंत : जो अनश्वर एवं अन्तहीन हैं

107. तारक : जीवों को मोक्ष प्रदान करने वाले

108. परमेश्वर : सर्वोच्च सत्ताधारी ईश्वर जिनसे सम्पूर्ण सृष्टि का सृजन एवं संहार होता है

108 Names of Lord Shiva

1.	Shiva	: Origin of purity
2.	Maheshwara	: Lord of Gods
3.	Shambhu	: one who gives prosperity
4.	Pinakin	: one who has a bow in his hand
5.	Shashi shekhar	: the God who has the crescent moon in his hair
6.	Vamadeva	: the God who is pleasing and auspicious in every way
7.	Virupaksha	: Lord Shiva with oblique eyes
8.	Kapardi	: the lord with thickly matted hair
9.	Nilalohita	: the one with red and blue colour
10.	Shankara	: one who bestows happiness and prosperity
11.	Shulapani	: the one who carries a trident
12.	Khatvangi	: the Lord who carries a knurled club (Khatvanga)

13. Vishnuvallabha	:	one who is dear to Lord Vishnu
14. Shipivishta	:	the Lord whose form emits great rays of light
15. Ambikanatha	:	Consort of Ambika (Parvati)
16. Shrikantha	:	Lord who has glorious neck
17. Bhaktavatsala	:	the one who is caring towards his devotees
18. Bhava	:	the Lord who is existence itself
19. Sharv	:	eradicator of all troubles
20. Trilokesha	:	the Lord of all the three worlds
21. Shitikantha	:	the Lord who has white neck
22. Shivapriya	:	Beloved of Parvati
23. Ugra	:	the one who is extremely fierce nature
24. Kapali	:	one who wears a necklace of skulls
25. Kamari	:	enemy of Kamadeva
26. Andhakasura Sudan	:	the Lord who killed the asura Andhakasur

27.	Gangadhara	: the God who holds the Ganges river in his head
28.	Lalataksha	: one who has an eye in the forehead
29.	Kalakala	: he is the death of death
30.	Kripanidhi	: the God who is the treasure of compassion
31.	Bheema	: the one who has fearful from
32.	Parshuhasta	: the God who holds axe in hands
33.	Mrigpaani	: the God who possess deer in hands
34.	Jattadhar	: the God who keeps tress (jata)
35.	Kailashavasi	: native of Kailasha
36.	Kawachi	: the God who possess armour
37.	Kathor	: the God who has a strong body
38.	Tripurantak	: the God who killed Tripurasur
39.	Vrishank	: the God who has a flag with a symbol of bull
40.	Vrishbharudh	: the one who rides bull

41. Bhasmodhulitavigrah : the one who applies ashes all over the body

42. Samapriya : the onc who loves equality

43. Swaramayi : the God who lives in all seven notes

44. Trayimurti : the one who is in veda form

45. Anishvara : the one who does not have any Lord

46. Sarvagya : the one who knows everything

47. Paramatma : Everyone's own soul

48. Somasuryaagnilochana : the one who has eyes in the form of Sun, Moon and Fire

49. Havi : the one who is offered as offering in the havan.

50. Yagyamaya : the architect of all sacrificial rites

51. Som : the one who includes the form of moon

52. Panchavaktra : one who has five faces

53. Sadashiva	:	the one who is eternally auspicious
54. Vishveshwara	:	Lord of the universe
55. Veerabhadra	:	who is violent and peaceful both
56. Gananatha	:	Lord of the ganas
57. Prajapati	:	the one who is the creator of dynasty
58. Hiranyareta	:	the one who emanates golden souls
59. Durdharsha	:	the one who is unconquerable
60. Girisha	:	God of mountains
61. Girisha	:	the God who sleeps on Kailash mountain
62. Anagha	:	who is pure
63. Bujangabhushana	:	Lord adorned with golden snakes
64. Bharga	:	who ends all sins
65. Giridhanva	:	God whose weapon is a mountain
66. Giripriya	:	one who is fond of mountains
67. Krittivasaa	:	God who wears clothes of tiger skin

68.	Purarati	:	destroyer of town or "Pur" named enemy
69.	Bhagwaan	:	Lord of prosperity
70.	Pramathadhipa	:	God who is served by Goblins
71.	Mrityunjaya	:	victor of death
72.	Sukshamatanu	:	God who has a minute body
73.	Jagadvyapi	:	God who dwells in the world
74.	Jagadguru	:	Guru of the whole earth
75.	Vyomakesh	:	Lord whose hair spreads in the sky
76.	Mahasenajanaka	:	father of Kartikeya
77.	Charuvikrama	:	conqueror of beauty
78.	Rudra	:	the one who gets sad by the pain of devotees
79.	Bhootapati	:	God of panchabhoota or bhootapreta
80.	Sthanu	:	firm and immovable Deity
81.	Ahirbhudhanya	:	the one who possess kundalini

82. Digambara : the God whose is the cosmos

83. Ashtamurti : Lord who has eight froms

84. Anekatma : the God who possess many forms

85. Satvika : Lord of boundless energy

86. Shuddhavigraha : Lord of pure soul

87. Shashvata : God who is eternal and endless

88. Khandaparshu : God who wears broken axe

89. Aja : the one who is boundless

90. Pashvimochana : Lord who releases all fetters

91. [illegible]da : the God who shows only mercy

92. Pashupati : Lord of animals

93. Deva : Lord of devas

94. Mahadeva : greatest of the Gods

95. Avayaya : the one who never subject to change

96. Hari : same as Lord Vishnu

97. Bhagnetrabhid : the God who damaged Bhaga's eye

98. Avayakt : Shiva who is unseen

99. Dakshadhwarahar : destroyer of Daksha's conceited sacrifice (yagya)

100. Har : the Lord who dissolves all bondage and sins

101. Pushadantabhit : one who punished pushan

102. Avyagra : God who is steady and unwavering

103. Sahsraksh : the one with thousand eyes

104. Sahasrapad : the lord who is standing and walking everywhere

105. Apavargaprad : God who gives and takes all things

106. Anant : the one God who is unending

107. Tarak : the God who is great liberator of mankind

108. Parameshwar : the Great Lord